T0196886

Get a Job in Space

Get a Job in Space is your one-stop-shop to learning everything there is to know about working in space... and the STEM subjects you need to get there!

From celestial science to intergalactic technology, discover what astronauts, technicians and engineers need to know to do their jobs. Would you rather study how plants grow on Mars than design a rocket? Explore your perfect career match, and dive into additional resources, classes and tips to help launch you into space.

This book is a must-have for kids fascinated by the cosmos, astronauts and the people who get them there.

Matt Koceich is a public school teacher with the Mansfield Independent School District. He has a Master's degree in Education from the University of North Texas and has been teaching for twenty-five years. He and his family live in Texas.

Get a Job in Space

A Kid's Guide to a Career in the Cosmos

Matt Koceich

Routledge
Taylor & Francis Group

NEW YORK AND LONDON

Cover image: © Getty Images

First published 2023
by Routledge
605 Third Avenue, New York, NY 10158

and by Routledge
4 Park Square, Milton Park, Abingdon, Oxon, OX14 4RN

Routledge is an imprint of the Taylor & Francis Group, an informa business

© 2023 Matt Koceich

The right of Matt Koceich to be identified as author of this work
has been asserted in accordance with sections 77 and 78 of the
Copyright, Designs and Patents Act 1988.

All rights reserved. No part of this book may be reprinted or
reproduced or utilized in any form or by any electronic, mechanical
or other means, now known or hereafter invented, including
photocopying and recording, or in any information storage or retrieval
system, without permission in writing from the publishers.

Trademark notice: Product or corporate names may be trademarks
or registered trademarks, and are used only for identification and
explanation without intent to infringe.

Library of Congress Cataloging-in-Publication Data
Names: Koceich, Matt (Public school teacher), author.
Title: Get a job in space : a kid's guide to a career in the cosmos /
Matt Koceich.
Description: New York, NY : Routledge, 2023. | Includes
bibliographical references. | Audience: Grades: 7-9 |
Summary—Provided by publisher.
Identifiers: LCCN 2022009123 (print) | LCCN 2022009124
(ebook) | ISBN 9781032200248 (paperback) | ISBN
9781032202990 (hardback) | ISBN 9781003263104 (ebook)
Subjects: LCSH: Astronautics—Vocational guidance—Juvenile
literature. | Space sciences—Vocational guidance—Juvenile
literature.
Classification: LCC TL850 .K63 2023 (print) | LCC TL850
(ebook) | DDC 629.450023—dc23/eng/20220615
LC record available at https://lccn.loc.gov/2022009123
LC ebook record available at https://lccn.loc.gov/2022009124

ISBN: 978-1-032-20299-0 (hbk)
ISBN: 978-1-032-20024-8 (pbk)
ISBN: 978-1-003-26310-4 (ebk)

DOI: 10.4324/9781003263104

Typeset in Palatino
by codeMantra

Contents

1

Help Wanted

By the time you reach your junior year of high school, you will have achieved so much. You will have passed so many tests and read so many books, and just thinking about all the homework you've done might make your brain hurt. Be proud of all that you've done!

However, there's still a big thing called college waiting for you and that's where your third year of high school comes in. That's the time when you should think about visiting colleges to see which one you like the best. However, to do that, it will help if you have an idea of what kind of job you want when you graduate.

No pressure! Seriously.

Your school days are to learn about what you like and what your talents are. Out of the billions of people in the world, there is only one you. That makes you very special. Maybe you like to draw or read books. Perhaps science just excites you like nothing else. Or maybe you like to play video games and hang out with your friends. There could be a chance you love a lot of different things. Remember, you are unique and that's the awesome part.

That's where this book comes to the rescue!

The goal of these pages is to not only give you information about careers related to the space industry, but to get you thinking about the cosmos in a brand new way. Hopefully, by the time you finish exploring all the cool opportunities here, you will give serious consideration to landing a job in the space field.

DOI: 10.4324/9781003263104-1

Even if you get to the end and feel that space is not what you're wired for, there's plenty of websites and links to keep your engaged well after you read the last page! So, if you're ready, let's go explore space!

T-MINUS...

When someone mentions the word *space*, what is the first thing that comes to mind? Mars? The Moon? Rockets and space shuttles? NASA? SpaceX? Or maybe it's galaxies and stars or planets and telescopes. Whatever you think about space, there's so much more! And when it comes to finding a career in the space industry, the possibilities are endless.

You may not have given much thought to what you want to do when you're older. Or maybe you are rather certain what your future career will be. Whether you're set on your career path in space or not, there's so much to learn about that you're in for a treat. You might discover a possible job that's just the right fit, or you might find a new way to use your talents and future job desires for a company that has connections to space.

In these pages, we'll explore a wide variety of careers that are connected to space. A lot of them you've probably heard of before and some of them you might be reading about for the first time. To make the best use of your time, QR codes have been inserted throughout the book for you to scan and learn more about various aspects of space.

At the end of the book, you'll find a section that lists colleges with degree plans that fit the space job you're looking for, as well as helpful links to websites that will assist you in landing an awesome space job. Don't worry. Even if you're not in high school, you can hold on to this book and pull it back out when you get there.

It might be a good idea to go grab a pen or pencil and new notebook to keep track of your learning. You never know when you'll be reading something and get a great idea! Taking notes or making doodle or drawings of your learning will help you connect more with the material. When there's a lot of information, it's easy to forget what you read, so jotting down your thoughts or pictures can help you remember what was important.

Ok. If you're ready, let's go!

Some of the highest profile space workers are astronauts and the teams of people who work behind the scenes to make space travel possible. The word astronaut comes from two Greek words meaning "space sailor." The first American astronauts worked way back in 1963. A lot has changed since then, but the quest for reaching out into our Milky Way galaxy has stayed the same.

Being an astronaut isn't all fun. There's a lot of hard work that goes with this prestigious career. Astronauts go through roughly twenty months of training which include flying airplanes and learning how to perform tasks in microgravity by suiting up and going into a pool of water to simulate how their bodies move in space-like conditions. Also, astronaut training includes becoming familiar with a mock-up of the International Space Station so the astronauts will know what to do when they get to the real one.

The first astronauts landed on the Moon back in 1969. They couldn't get there without the help of important women mathematicians who calculated flight trajectories for the *Mercury* missions; Katherine Johnson, Dorothy Vaughan and Mary Jackson were all featured in the popular 2016 movie *Hidden Figures*. Technology has come a long way since then, but the role of astronauts and the crews that help them behind the scenes are still just as important as ever.

MORE DOORS

If being an astronaut doesn't sound interesting, there are so many more jobs to consider. Maybe you don't want to travel into space yourself, but doing something like building a telescope that does is more exciting. Astronomers are always observing objects within the universe, including planets, stars and galaxies. They may rely on Earth-based equipment, such as telescopes, or on space-based equipment, such as probes, to collect data on celestial bodies. Analyzing the data they collect provides clues to some questions, such as the age of certain planets.

There was a famous American astronomer named Edwin Hubble who discovered that what scientists thought were clouds and gas were actually galaxies way beyond our own Milky Way. NASA named the Hubble Space Telescope in his honor. The Hubble telescope was launched into low Earth orbit and has been in operation ever since. With its awesome views of the universe, Hubble has captured over a million pictures of stars, galaxies and planets that have captivated the imaginations of people all over the world (NASA, 2022, *About Edwin Hubble*).

More recently, in December of 2021, NASA launched its largest and most powerful ever James Webb telescope. It is traveling about a million miles away from Earth to begin its orbit around the Sun where it will begin to study the stars and galaxies.

Consider another possibility of starting your very own space company like Elon Musk did. He is the very popular engineer who created SpaceX (you may also know that he created the Tesla car too!). His company makes engines and rockets that send astronauts up to the International Space Station. Musk said his goal is to get men and women on Mars in the not too distant future. SpaceX has a growing launch site in Boca Chica, TX, called Starbase. Starbase is near Brownsville and is where teams of highly trained professionals produce rockets and test them. Scan the QR code to check out an awesome YouTube channel devoted to covering everything Starbase. Be warned, it's addicting! Hopefully, you'll see something that sparks your curiosity. When it comes to space, your possibilities are endless.

NASA, or the National Aeronautics and Space Administration, is another great place to find a ton of space jobs. They have twenty facilities across the United States and employ over 17,000 people. Most of those jobs never leave Earth. Two of their main locations are Cape Canaveral in Florida where a lot of rocket launches take place, and the Johnson Space Center in Houston, Texas. The Johnson Space Center is a great place you can visit and learn a lot about NASA and take a cool tour of their facilities, including mission control.

Switching gears, here's a space path you might not have heard about. It's called atmospheric science. Atmospheric scientists, including meteorologists, observe weather and climate. They prepare long- and short-term forecasts by analyzing data from computer programs and from instruments such as weather balloons, radar systems and satellite images. These scientists also may study atmospheric phenomena, such as the Northern Lights and trade winds.

Have you ever heard of a plasma physicist? Sounds pretty cool. These scientists study plasmas, which occur naturally both in interplanetary space and in stars. Plasma, very hot gas that has a ton of energy, is considered the fourth state of matter after solids, liquids and gasses. These professionals help us understand the universe as well as our everyday lives. For example, plasma physicists may study the interaction between the Sun and Earth to improve space-weather forecasts, which may help to protect satellites, power transmissions and aircraft communication systems.

Do you like building things? Engineers play a great role in the space industry. Not only do engineers build the rockets that travel into space, they also construct instruments that look for water on Mars. Engineers have endless opportunities when it comes to getting a job in space. A lot of colleges offer engineering degrees, so this is a niche where you won't have a hard time finding work.

Do you like taking pictures? Photographers in the space industry process the pictures captured by astronauts and satellites and turn them into pieces that capture the amazing beauty of the universe. That's a really cool responsibility and would provide a constant opportunity to learn new things about space.

Then there are technicians. These men and women are very important to space missions. A typical spacecraft will go through more than 200 tests to make sure nothing's wrong and that the ship will perform flawlessly once launched. That's a huge responsibility if you're up for the challenge!

We mentioned engineers, but there's a specific one called a radio frequency engineer. Radio frequency engineers design, construct and maintain the wireless communication systems aboard spacecraft. Radio frequency signals are how spaceships talk to mission control, so this would be an essential position you might want to consider.

Mission control specialists are the people who help the astronauts do their jobs. Mission control is divided into flight control and ground control. Ground control crews gather data from the space craft and the launch sights and hand it over to flight control teams who then analyze the information to come up with plans and procedures to make sure everything runs smoothly.

Finally, here are some other really cool space jobs to consider as you get closer to choosing a career. How about becoming a cyber architect? This job works to protect space vehicles from cyber attacks. As a cyber architect, you would come up with creative solutions to prevent the attacks as well as research where potential vulnerabilities might be and help keep everything safe. That sounds awesome!

Or what about computers? Do you like coding? Do you think you might be interested in creating games or stories? Software developers make the programs that run all the systems needed to ensure rocket launches run smoothly. Computers need the software to run and since everything runs on computers you can be sure this job is one you will keep for a long time.

Recently, our country added a new military branch called the Space Force! From Space Operations Officers who monitor and command satellites to Cyber Warfare Operations Officers who command cyberspace weapons systems like combat communications, missile guidance systems, rocket launches and even our country's power grid, Space Force has it all. Their tagline is *The Sky Is Not the Limit*, which makes sense because when it comes to space, the possibilities are indeed endless.

THE NEXT BIG THING

Plans are already underway to get people to Mars in the not-so-distant future. And to do that, space agencies like NASA and SpaceX are working together to dream up ways to get humans back to the Moon, and from there the thirty-four million miles out to the red planet of Mars, which would translate into six months of travel time!

NASA has their Artemis program that is working on not only getting people to the Moon, but also constructing a Gateway that will act like a mini space station as it stays in lunar orbit. The goal of the Gateway is to allow humans to live for months in space as they make multiple trips down to the Moon's surface for research on soil samples and other findings.

Δ

This chapter has covered a lot of cool jobs that have something to do with space. Was there one in particular that resonated with you? Remember, it's okay if you're not sure. Think about connecting your talents with different aspects of space careers, and before you know it you'll be on your way to finding the job you were born to do!

Did you jot anything down in your notebook? Why don't you take a second and draw a picture of something in this chapter that really caught your attention? It would be fun to make notes in the margins of your picture about how you could use your talents to upgrade what's already being done.

One quick note before we move on. By now, you've probably heard of STEM (science, technology, engineering and math). Your school and tons of others across the country make sure to focus on these subjects because they know how important they are to students. For example, if you're thinking about becoming an astronaut, you have to earn a Master's degree (five years of college) in a STEM discipline. In the next chapter, we're going to start with *science* and hone in on how specifically it is used in the space industry.

2

Celestial Science

When you think of science class, what comes to mind? The water cycle? Plant cells? Planets? Beakers and bar graphs? There's physical science, life science, Earth and space science, investigations and tons of question asking.

When it comes to space, there's a special place where people get to study all kinds of science called the International Space Station (ISS). It's like something out of Star Wars! Imagine a ton of your school's science labs all connected, but up in space, 248 miles above you, orbiting the Earth at a blistering speed of five miles per second! Can you believe that? It takes the ISS about ninety minutes to orbit the Earth one time. That's fast!

HISTORY OF THE ISS

Back in 1984, our country had a president named Ronald Reagan who first directed NASA to begin construction on a space station over the following ten years. That directive finally became reality in 1998, when the first module *Unity* was launched into orbit. We had rockets back then called space shuttles that actually carried the module into space. In 2000, the first people (one American astronaut and two Russian cosmonauts) stayed on the International Space Station for several months. In 2001, *Destiny* was launched and became part of the station and served as the primary lab (NASA, 2022, *International Space Station*).

DOI: 10.4324/9781003263104-2

Fast forward to 2008, when two more modules, or sections, were added to the station. The first, named *Columbus*, was added from the European Space Agency while the second, *Kibo*, was a Japanese lab module. Along the way, more modules were added, making the entire station as big as a football field (including the endzones), weighing over 800,000 pounds! It has massive solar arrays that capture the Sun's light and convert it into electricity. There are over 260,000 solar cells altogether that provide more than enough energy to power the ISS. That's enough electricity to power forty homes back here on Earth!

The space station is a massive work of art and engineering. Scan the QR code to check out a really detailed diagram that shows all the different pieces of the station as well as a list of cool facts and figures.

What about the fascinating research that's conducted aboard the space station? Remember that one of the main goals of space exploration is being able to sustain life on our Moon and eventually Mars. The effects of microgravity on the human body are a key area of research that scientists are interested in studying. For example, did you know that when a person is in space for a long period of time, their muscles atrophy, or lose mass? Or how about this bizarre fact: astronauts lose about one to two percent of their bone mineral density every month they're in space. That may not be an issue while they're in space, but when they return to Earth, they run the risk of experiencing bone fractures. Bones, like muscles, are able to change depending on how they're used.

And then there's the topic of plants. Right now, there is a working vegetable garden aboard the ISS! It's small (about the size of a carry-on piece of luggage) and can hold up to six plants at a time. Each plant grows in a "pillow" that holds the roots and soil. Water, nutrients and air are carefully given to the plant inside the pillow device so that it will be able to live and grow in space. Lettuce and cabbage have been some of the veggies that the space station has successfully grown! (Anthony, 2022)

What do you think you would want to grow in space? What might be some problems that you would have to solve in order to make your plant prosper? Take a second to jot your ideas down in your notebook. You might be on to something!

Another cool job is to study how liquids behave in space. Maybe you've seen videos of water droplets floating around. Because of microgravity, more droplets are able to hold together to form a big blob of water. Fluids in space don't follow the same rules as they do back here on Earth. When you think about a car, gas flows from the tank to a fuel pump that pushes the gas into the engine. That wouldn't work the same way in space. This is a neat example of what you could research if you took a job in space.

From the way it was constructed to all the cool experiments carried out in its labs, the International Space Station is truly amazing. Scan the QR code to unlock an awesome link with pictures and fun facts about the International Space Station.

The future of the International Space Station is uncertain. What is certain is that in 2024, funding for the hundred billion dollar project will come to an end. There is talk of opening up ownership of the ISS to private companies, but that option isn't set in stone. A lot of people believe that the ISS is vital for research that will help with future Moon landings as well as sustaining life on Mars, while others think that all the money to operate the station could be better spent back here on Earth. Whatever the outcome, the ISS has been a great resource for scientists to carry out microgravity experiments.

SCIENTIFIC METHOD

Where else in space does science come into the picture?

The Sun is a great starting point because there are so many things to study when it comes to our planet's primary energy source! One thing scientists study are solar winds and how they cause things called auroras. Basically, the Sun gives off charged particles that interact with the upper layers of Earth's atmosphere and create beautiful light displays like the Northern Lights. When you think about the Sun, can you see yourself in the future working with a team to use its power to make life on Earth better? What questions do you have about the Sun?

Mars is another huge area where science and space collide. One of the biggest things that scientists are trying to figure out is whether or not life ever existed on the red planet. Climate is another area that scientists are studying to see if life could exist on Mars in the future. To piggyback on that research, scientists study things like radiation levels to make sure if astronauts do make it to Mars they would be safe. Could you ever see yourself living on Mars one day?

There are different fields of science when we talk about space. Astronomy, for example, deals with the study of planets, comets, stars and galaxies. How cool would that be to have a job doing that all day long? There was a man by the name of Galileo Galilei who loved astronomy and made major improvements to the telescope and was able to discover Sun spots as well as the four major moons of Jupiter that bear his name. There's different divisions within the field of astronomy, like observational astronomy that deals with the things in space we can see, or solar astronomy which deals primarily with studying all things related to the Sun. Planetary astronomy studies the planets, comets, asteroids and moons, while stellar astronomy studies things like red giants, supernovas, black holes and neutron stars. Finally, astrometry is a branch of astronomy that deals with the measurements, positions and locations of stars.

How about astrobiology? That's the study of life in outer space. Can you picture yourself in a job doing that? It seems like our planet is the only one with life, but believe it or not, scientists have found traces of liquid water on two of Jupiter's moons: Europa and Ganymede, as well as on two of Saturn's moons, Titan and Enceladus. It is too cold to support life on these moons' surfaces, but people believe there might be underground oceans there that may have supported life in the past and may do so in the present. Currently, there are two rovers on Mars, *Curiosity* and

Perseverance, that are trying to find evidence of ancient life and rivers. Do you think aliens exist somewhere else in our universe?

Planetary science deals with studying the planets, but not just the ones you learned about in third grade. Not only have scientists sent probes to all the planets you know about, but they have discovered things called exoplanets which are planets that exist outside of our solar system.

Ready for this? There are places in the universe where scientists believe planets might contain forms of life! Tau Ceti is a star like our Sun, located twelve light years away, and has five planets that orbit it (Wall, 2015). Two of those planets are in what people call the habitable zone, meaning conditions for life are similar to our own Earth!

Astrophysics deals with how planets and stars work and studies concepts like dark matter, black holes and other celestial bodies. Cosmology deals with the origin of our universe, its evolution, as well as its fate, and astronautics deals with the science of space travel.

Space medicine is where doctors work to take care of the health and safety of astronauts. Aerospace physicians also have to consider mental health because of the way astronauts endure long periods of time away from their families as well as the very close living quarters aboard the spaceships.

Those are a ton of unique options for future careers. Did any of those jump out at you? Don't forget to make notes along the way! Let's take a look at another cool possibility for you to pursue when you're considering jobs after college.

REARVIEW MIRROR

In your parents' car, there are a few mirrors that help them see what's going on behind the car. The mirrors keep you safe when driving to make sure it's okay to switch lanes. There's actually a cool branch of space science that deals with looking back at Earth and making observations to gather important information about our precious planet.

For example, scientists use satellites to gather data to determine more accurate maps of the Earth's surface as well as how the inside of the Earth is structured. Studying Earth from space has helped scientists understand more about how the Earth rotates and moves and the movement of the tides and oceans. Another term you might have heard of is climate change. Scientists are using important data collected from satellites to understand the causes and effects of this area of concern.

Weather patterns on our planet are another thing that is studied from space. Scientists use the data collected in space to not only track weather but also to predict or forecast it. That's really helpful because people can use that information to stay safe, like avoiding hurricanes that are a constant threat in our country during the summer months.

Pokemon Go is a popular gaming app that relies on GPS (Global Positioning System) technology. Originally created for military use, GPS technology makes our life easier with apps like Waze that helps drivers know where to go by providing real-time maps of traffic flow and patterns. Campers, hikers, fishermen and people that run airlines all rely on this epic invention that starts in space.

Another area of space-to-Earth science comes in a term called remote sensing. This is when scientists use satellites to observe characteristics of land and water surfaces to gather information to make better maps, discover where important minerals are located, what the best use of the land is, and how to manage our planet's key resources from the conditions of crops and patterns of pollution (Earth Data, 2021).

Remember, whether you love science, or maybe up to now it hasn't been on your list of favorite school subjects, your future might involve a career in space. Either way, all the opportunities to get involved with science on the International Space Station really make it a subject to pay attention to.

Don't forget, you are special and unique, so whatever you put your mind to, you will be able to add new things and ideas! Spend time thinking about what you would like to research about the International Space Station. You never know. One day you might have the chance to make your ideas come true.

There are so many options to choose from when considering a career in space. It might be helpful to mark your place here and grab your notebook again and journal your thoughts and ideas about space. Draw pictures. Jot down ideas. Concepts. Make it your own.

In the next chapter, we're going to investigate ways that technology is used for space-related jobs. Ready? Let's go.

3

Intergalactic Technology

When it comes to technology in space, the possibilities are end-less. Sometimes people think of technology as the bits and pieces that go into a smartphone to make it "smart." If you're keeping a journal to record your thoughts about possible careers in space you might like to pursue when you're older, start a new section for the way your talents or ideas might line up with the informa-tion provided here in Chapter 3.

Let's start with a look at some major spacecraft that have been launched to learn how technology plays an important part in successful missions. We'll travel back to the beginning of NA-SA's journey to space and look at the Mercury program. Started in 1958, the Mercury project was the first US man-in-space effort. From 1961 to 1963, Mercury made a total of six manned space flights. To get an astronaut in space orbiting the Earth was the primary goal of the Mercury missions (Smithsonian, 2022).

The Mercury spaceship was a one-man capsule that was equipped with a heat shield to protect the astronauts against the 3,000 degree heat upon reentry into the Earth's atmosphere. The rocket booster that launched the Mercury ship was called Atlas and was about ninety-three feet tall and ten feet wide. That's small compared to the other ships we'll be looking at later on, but the cool thing is it all started with a dream. Then someone sketched out the dream on paper and before long a space career was made!

DOI: 10.4324/9781003263104-3

What kind of spaceship would you design? How many astronauts would it carry? How tall would it be? Take a moment to sketch out your thoughts! And don't worry about perfection. Just getting your ideas down on paper is enough. You'll be surprised at how many new ideas you'll have after putting your first one out there.

The next capsule designed by NASA was called Gemini and allowed for two astronauts inside. It was designed to function at a higher level because it had to remain in space longer and needed maneuvering capabilities to dock with another spacecraft. Gemini would have to move in all different directions in its orbital path. Gemini also required the first onboard computers to calculate the complicated docking maneuvers. The Gemini was launched on a Titan II rocket that was roughly ten feet longer than its Atlas predecessor (Wilson, 2022).

It's really exciting to think that you might have the next rocket design in your imagination. Take some time to work on your rocket drawing. You never know what you can create if you don't try!

For more interesting ways technology advanced when it comes to spacecraft we now turn our attention to the famous Apollo missions which were powered by the epic Saturn V rockets.

The Apollo capsule sat three astronauts and made a total of six Moon landings, and included the Lunar Module which carried two astronauts from the command module down to the surface of the Moon. It had a rocket of its own that allowed it to blast off of the Moon's surface and rejoin the command module in space. The Saturn V was the tallest, heaviest and most powerful of all of NASA's rockets. It was 363 feet tall and thirty-three feet in diameter and came in at over six million pounds. That's massive! Doesn't that give you some inspiration as you design a rocket of your own?

Moving on, we come to the Space Shuttle program that lasted from 1981 all the way to 2011. The iconic shuttle took the technology of the previous spaceships and added a few little cool twists for a new generation of astronauts. The shuttle was designed to hold eight astronauts and resembled a huge airplane with a gigantic cargo bay that was capable of holding up to 50,000 pounds. When the shuttle reentered Earth's orbit, it would act as a glider and land by the pull of gravity.

It was propelled by two external solid rocket boosters (each giving the rocket 400,000 pounds of thrust) and a million pound fuel tank. Although half the height of Saturn V, the space shuttle packed a punch when it came to space missions. In all, the shuttle made 135 missions in its thirty years flying into space.

The shuttle was a super complex flying machine and required a ton of technology to make it work. One of the biggest advances with the shuttle was the reusable engines. Before the shuttle, the engines were called "one and done," but you can imagine how much money is saved when the engines can be reused. Another advance with the shuttle was with its flight system called "fly by wire." Before the shuttle, pilot controls were linked directly to wing and tail surfaces in order to control the spacecraft.

The new "fly by wire" technology had computer systems that helped control the massive ship in case weather or other factors like wind threatened the flight. Perhaps the most iconic technological advance on the space shuttle was the black tiles that made up the thermal protection system. Each shuttle had over 20,000 tiles that kept heat away from the spaceship when it reentered our atmosphere.

Let's pause here and think about your ideas. Where are you with your drawing? Notice how advances in technology with NASA's rockets helped each mission accomplish bigger things. What kind of technology will your rocket have? What will it look like? How many astronauts will be able to travel on your space vehicle? Make sure your design will incorporate reusable systems to save money.

Let's move on to a company you've most likely heard of, SpaceX. Engineer Elon Musk has invented some cool things in his fifty years on the planet. You may know that he's the brains behind the Tesla electric car as well as the owner of SpaceX. Elon's team has created the Falcon 9 rocket which is the very first orbital class reusable rocket. The Falcon stands 229 feet tall and twelve feet wide. Its engines generate 1.7 million pounds of thrust. The Dragon capsule that sits atop the Falcon can hold up to seven astronauts.

The other big thing from SpaceX is called the Starship. This is the ship that Elon hopes will take astronauts to the Moon and then on to Mars. Starship will be 390 feet tall and thirty feet in diameter. Using Raptor engines, Starship will have double the amount of thrust that Saturn V had as well as double the amount of thrust of the Falcon 9.

Finally, SpaceX has deployed Starlink satellites to provide customers on Earth with reliable broadband Internet service from space. The company hopes to reach people who live in remote areas of the world to help them have better connection to the Internet.

We already talked about the International Space Station, but as of April 2021, the Chinese have launched their own space station called *Tiangong*, which translates to "heavenly palace." There are plans to carry out a myriad of experiments on Tiangong, and it's exciting to know this new station will be in operation for years to come.

Have you ever talked to someone who didn't live anywhere near you? Maybe they lived in another state or country. It's amazing how technology helps us communicate over long distances, and space is no different. NASA has technology called the Deep Space Network which allows them to talk to astronauts on space missions and receive information from the Voyager 1 and 2 spacecraft. These craft were launched way back in 1977 and have studied Jupiter, Saturn, Uranus and Neptune.

So how is something so far away able to send information across the universe? There are these massive radio antennas located in different parts of the world. The largest one is 230 feet in diameter! People back here on Earth collect the data and photos to be used for future planning. Is there something in your mind that could help in this area? Think about it and jot some ideas down in your notebook. You never know how one sketch now can turn into reality later on in your life. Go for it! Dream big and use your brain to reach for the stars!

Interstellar travel between stars and planetary systems is still in the theory stage, but you might have an idea that helps future scientists and astronauts find a way to go beyond where any human has ever gone. Making engines work to provide propulsion is very different in space than it is on Earth. Nuclear propulsion and beam-powered propulsion are two viable options for this type of galactic exploration in the future. Google them and see how you can incorporate them in your spaceship design.

A cool thing to think about is how your ideas about how to use technology in space can eventually be used to help people back here on Earth. For example, the cameras astronauts use to take pictures of the Earth from space use the same technology as our smartphones. Back in the 1990s, NASA built a new low-power sensor, using a complementary metal oxide semiconductor (CMOS). This CMOS technology is used all throughout our devices, making it possible for cell phone cameras to produce high-quality pictures and videos (Wikitronics, 2022).

Have you been at a friend's house and seen an air purifier? This is another thing people use to keep the air inside their homes clean from bacteria and other things that we don't need to be breathing in. Thanks to NASA, we have these helpful devices available to use in our homes. NASA first researched a machine to help plants grow strong in space. It worked extremely well at getting rid of toxins in the air and now has been adapted into the purifiers that keep the air we breathe cleaner.

NASA technologies even help companies like Speedo design more effective swimsuits. NASA does a ton of research on a concept called viscous drag which is the force of friction that slows down a moving object through things like air or water. They took this knowledge and applied what they know about fluid dynamics and helped reduce viscous drag in Speedo's new LZR Racer suit.

Back in the early 1970s, food company Pillsbury took drastic measures to alter the safety controls for its food production after finding shards of glass in one of its baby cereals. The company had a research scientist who worked with NASA to develop ways to keep food safe for astronauts who might not eat it until weeks after it was made. Because of this hard work a process was created called Hazard Analysis and Critical Control Point. Today, this is a common program which ensures that food is safe for people to consume.

And then we can't forget about tools. They're everywhere. Cordless power tools make life easier, and NASA technology helped these inventions come to life. When the Apollo program was in full swing, they realized their astronauts needed to be able to work in space and on the Moon, where you don't have electrical outlets. Black & Decker, the company that invented cordless power tools, worked with NASA to develop battery operated tools that were useful for astronauts as well as their consumers.

Another area where NASA technology has helped people get jobs done more efficiently is with farming. John Deere, the famous green and yellow tractor company, uses GPS receivers linked to NASA's global network of ground stations to enable self-guided tractors and to give farmers an accurate mapping of their crops.

WHAT'S NEXT?

Does your school have a robotics club? Have you ever played with a remote-controlled car? The future of space technology will be loaded with robots. Scientists predict that within this century, our entire solar system will be explored and mapped by tons of microscopic robotic craft, interacting with each other like a flock of birds. Giant robotic fabricators will be able to build huge solar energy collectors in space and explore the outer planets. To accomplish this, they will have to utilize AI technology to make autonomous decisions because it takes too long for radio signals to travel between Earth and the outer planets.

That was a lot of awesome information about how technology is used in space. Spend some time jotting down any ideas you might have after reading all the information in this chapter. You'll be surprised at what you can create. Don't forget, you can always go back and reread sections to pick up more information that you might have missed the first time.

When you're ready, our next chapter is going to help you explore jobs that combine engineering and space!

4

Out of This World Engineering

So far in our journey to learn about different jobs people do in and for space, we've come across some pretty cool careers. Remember, the goal of this book is to get you thinking about your talents and how they might connect to one or more aspects of space. Hopefully you found a notebook to keep all your doodles and great ideas in. If you haven't, why not find one now and dive into your awesome imagination? You'll be amazed at what you can create. And you never know what kind of sketch you make now could turn out to be the invention that revolutionizes the space industry in the future.

Aerospace engineering is the main career path when it comes to making things soar into orbit. So what do aerospace engineers do? They develop state-of-the-art technologies and incorporate them into aerospace vehicle systems. These creations are used for transportation, communications, exploration and defense. This involves the design and manufacturing of spacecraft and the propulsion systems needed to launch them into space, as well as satellites and missiles. Successful aerospace engineers know all about aerodynamics, materials and structures, propulsion and vehicle dynamics. That sounds like a really cool job to be a part of!

An aerospace engineer designs, tests, and manages the manufacturing of aircraft, spacecraft, satellites and missiles. They also work on developing new technologies to be used in space exploration, aviation and defense systems. Aerospace engineers also have the ability to work on specialized projects, like missiles

DOI: 10.4324/9781003263104-4

and rockets, military fighter jets, spacecraft, helicopters or commercial aircraft like the kind you see at an airport. They may also choose to specialize in designing instrumentation which would be the control panels and interface buttons used to steer the ship. Other projects include figuring out communication, navigation and guidance systems that go on to be used in space.

A lot of what an aerospace engineer looks at is doing research and testing of their designs. There's a ton of fancy words that go along with engineering and space, like aerodynamics, thermodynamics, celestial mechanics, flight mechanics, propulsion, acoustics, and guidance and control systems. It might sound like a foreign language now, but as you get older and do more research you'll have a great understanding of all the things that go into aerospace engineering.

Spacecraft may include products such as: rockets, remote sensing satellites, missiles, space launchers, space vehicles, navigational systems and planetary probes. Aerospace engineers also like to investigate, which means they love to think. They work with computers and sophisticated software programs which assist with design elements. These software programs build virtual models, and it is up to the aerospace engineer to run test simulations and perform evaluations before the manufacturing process begins.

WHO'S WHO?

Engineers are curious about how things work. They love to figure out solutions to problems.

You've probably heard of a man who lived a long time ago named Leonardo DaVinci. He loved to draw things and he had a mind that always wondered how machines could work in the future. One of his most famous ideas was of a flying machine he called an ornithopter. It looked like a big wooden bird, with a wing span of more than thirty-three feet. He did this in 1485 when he really got into studying birds. The idea was that a person would lie down on a wooden plank and operate levers and pulleys to make the wings work.

Engineers who work with rockets and spaceships deal with four concepts: weight, lift, drag and thrust. These are not just a random set of words. In fact, engineer George Cayley in 1799 figured out and identified these four forces which act on heavier-than-air flying machines. It was his ideas and research that helped the Wright brothers become the first people to fly a fixed-wing plane at Kitty Hawk, North Carolina.

There was another engineer named Igor Sikorsky who invented the helicopter. It wasn't easy and he experienced a ton of failure, but the inspiring thing is he didn't quit. It took thirty whole years for Sikorsky to see his helicopter invention come to life, but he stuck with the hard work and tons of hours of effort and was finally able to see his dream come true.

Robert H. Goddard is known in the aerospace world as the father of modern rocket propulsion. In 1926, he was the first person to design and launch a liquid fuel rocket that looked like a piece of playground equipment for kids to climb on at recess rather than a powerful machine that would one day be the basis for future space flight (Lehman, 2021).

In 1938, an engineer by the name of James Hart Wyld created a rocket that would eventually power a plane to go faster than the speed of sound. Werner von Braun was a German aerospace engineer who came to the United States in the 1960s and helped NASA create the Saturn V super heavy launch vehicle that we learned about earlier (Stanzione, 2019).

Kalpana Chawla was an engineer and astronaut and the first person of Indian origin to travel to space. She flew aboard the Space Shuttle Columbia in 1997 where she was in charge of operating the shuttle's robotic arm. In 2003, she was on the Columbia shuttle again and tragically lost her life when the spaceship exploded on reentry into the Earth's atmosphere (Tillman, 2022).

All of these people and a host of others all started with an idea. They took the idea and turned it into reality. What are you interested in? What in your world do you see that could help you with your space inventions? Don't forget to write down your observations. Draw some simple sketches and you'll be on your way to thinking up the next big thing to help space travel become a better experience in the future!

DO WHAT?

Engineering is a really cool career path. When you combine that with space missions awesome things happen. High-performance space systems such as space vehicles and instruments, sensors, actuators, mechanisms, propulsion rockets and vehicle control by using state-of-the-art technology is the daily norm. What a job!

Engineers work to create complex space vehicles like launchers, satellites and deep space probes just to name a few. Spacecraft system development includes design, development, integration, verification/testing and operation. That's a ton of work to keep you busy and always give you something new. Engineers are also responsible for working in multidisciplinary design teams to formulate spacecraft systems that work.

Talk about responsibility. Engineers have to design, develop, construct, test and operate vehicles that are used in space like launchers and satellites that travel around Earth and other planetary bodies as well as in outer space. A big part of this work deals with space systems. This focuses on the architectural development of launchers, ground control, orbits and constellations, payloads and mission operations.

Space propulsion / rocket systems are vital to any space mission. Research projects in this field encompass rocket stages and rocket propulsion systems. If you are interested in designing and building machines that fly, this career may be the right choice for you!

ORION!

For the first time in a generation, NASA is building a human spacecraft for deep-space missions! Orion will travel to the Moon and hopefully Mars! Named after one of the largest constellations in the night sky and drawing from more than fifty years of spaceflight research and development, the Orion spacecraft is designed to take astronauts to deep space for years to come. Orion will serve as the exploration vehicle carrying crews to space, sustain astronauts during their missions and provide safe reentry from deep space return velocities.

Orion missions will launch from NASA's Kennedy Space Center in Florida on the agency's new, powerful heavy-lift rocket, the Space Launch System (SLS). The first mission, Artemis I, won't have any astronauts aboard, but will travel thousands of miles past the Moon over the course of three weeks. The missions with astronauts should be lifting off within the next few years.

IN THE WORKS

What are NASA engineers working on these days? For starters, the Artemis project is challenging engineers to land the first woman on the Moon and to explore more of the lunar surface than ever before. A huge goal of this endeavor is to establish the first long-term presence on the Moon. Then, NASA will take the information they learn from this operation to send the first astronauts to Mars!

A massive job for engineers has been creating the Space Launch System. As mentioned, this is the rocket that will power the Artemis missions. Getting to the Moon requires a powerful rocket ship to do two things: accelerate fast enough to get past the pull of Earth's gravity, and set it on a precise trajectory to wherever NASA needs it to go. When the Space Launch System takes off on its first flight it will produce over eight million pounds of thrust! That's more than any rocket ever!

All that power doesn't come at once. Engineers have to figure out ways to spread the power over several sections, or stages. At liftoff, the first stage, the SLS core and twin solid rocket boosters will fire and propel the nearly six million pound Orion rocket off the launch pad and send it speeding into orbit. All of this will happen in eight minutes as SLS's four RS-25 engines burn 735,000 gallons of liquid propellant to create two million pounds of thrust. The twin rocket boosters will burn more than two million pounds of solid propellant to create more than seven million pounds of thrust (Garcia, 2022). The numbers are mind blowing!

Next, when all the fuel of the first stage is gone, the core and boosters get dropped and fall away. The interim cryogenic propulsion stage fires its RL10 engine setting up the next phase of the mission. At this point, the upper part of the rocket and Orion are soaring almost 100 miles above Earth, accelerating at more than 17,500 miles per hour, and beginning a circular orbit around Earth. Deep space missions require rockets that can travel beyond low Earth orbit and send the spacecraft even farther out to reach the Moon.

TRANS-LUNAR INJECTION

How is that for a fancy phrase? This is the key move that makes it possible to send Orion 280,000 miles beyond Earth to the Moon! The trans-lunar injection maneuver will begin as the upper part of the rocket produces 24,750 pounds of thrust to accelerate the vehicle to more than 24,500 miles per hour, a velocity fast enough to get the rocket past the pull of gravity and on toward the Moon's gravity.

When its time on the lunar surface is done and Orion heads home, one of the most crucial tests occurs. Engineers have worked hard on creating a shield that will allow Orion to endure temperatures as high as 5,000 degrees Fahrenheit during reentry into Earth's atmosphere. With the help of the Navy, NASA will then recover Orion from the Pacific Ocean off the coast of California. Then everyone will be able to celebrate this truly historic feat!

FARTHER THAN EVER

The next step for space engineering will be to start sending people on bold missions beyond the Moon all the way out to Mars! This type of mission has never been done before, but the possibilities of such an event are inspiring. And who knows, by the time we are ready to send astronauts safely to Mars, you might be old enough to be working and have your own career helping create these awesome rockets and systems.

To land larger cargos on the Moon and to send people to Mars, SLS will evolve to a configuration called Block 1B. This rocket configuration will use a powerful stage called Exploration Upper instead of the interim cryogenic propulsion stage. The ultimate evolution of SLS is the Block 2 rocket that will be able to carry either astronauts and cargo or just cargo needed for Mars exploration or for planetary missions that will head to the outer solar system.

The possibilities are endless. With the information you learned in this chapter, now would be a good time to revisit your notebook and jot down some more ideas you have for building structures on Mars that would help sustain life once these powerful machines have taken the astronauts there. How amazing would it be if your ideas were the ones that were used to turn space travel dreams into reality!

You don't have to wait until you're in high school to begin dreaming of all the ways your unique talents can be used to help people explore the infinite regions of space. Starting now, you have special skills you can practice honing that will help you as you build your knowledge and understanding. Read and research along the way, and you'll be surprised at how much you'll learn by the time you get to high school.

In the next chapter, we are going to look at different ways math is used in space. Math may be a subject you've never had a big interest in, but read on and see how cool it can be, especially when it comes to space.

5

Heavenly Math

Numbers are everywhere, and when it comes to space the same holds true. Astronauts use math all the time when going on their space exploration missions. Let's take one example of how math is crucial when it comes to traveling in space.

On Earth, when someone wants to fly a plane from point A to point B, a straight line is always the fastest route. Recently, mathematicians and NASA engineers have learned that to work with gravity and conserve fuel, it may be necessary to make bizarre loops through space. For example, there was a spacecraft called Genesis that had been in space for two years collecting solar particles. When it was time to return to Earth, instead of coming straight back, Genesis took a long curvy path, going past Earth on a million-mile loop to save fuel by using the power of the Earth-Sun gravitational pull.

Scientists and engineers design space probes that travel between planets by taking advantage of the different gravitational tugs of different planets and moons. These tugs save tons of fuel and allow the probes to go huge distances. Without advances in math, this awesome way of space travel would not have been found.

When people think about going to space, they usually think about going up. And that's certainly true, but it's only part of the story. It's sort of hard to define exactly where the atmosphere ends and outer space begins (since the atmosphere gradually falls off as you go up in altitude), but one popular choice is the

DOI: 10.4324/9781003263104-5

so-called "Karman line" at a height of sixty-two miles above sea level. A lot of people are surprised to find that space begins only 100 km up… since that's really not that far. But the problem with getting there is that it's "uphill" the whole way, which means you have to fight gravity the whole time.

Getting up that high is only half the battle of getting into orbit around the Earth. Because if you fly a spacecraft straight up into the sky and then cut the engines, it will simply come right back down to the ground. If your goal is to get a satellite into orbit around the Earth or to deliver a person to the International Space Station, the rocket doesn't just need to get into space, it needs to stay there. And that means it needs to end up flying sideways really, *really* fast—around 18,000 miles per hour! A rocket or satellite traveling that fast completes one orbit every ninety minutes. That's lightning fast considering it takes five hours to fly across the United States in an airplane. It takes a rocket in orbit only ten minutes to fly across the United States.

ROUND AND ROUND

But why does a rocket or satellite or space station need to be moving sideways so fast to stay in orbit? The answer has to do with a certain type of math called geometry. As you know, the Earth is roughly spherical. While it's possible to go around the Earth in an elliptical orbit, think about the simple case of a perfectly circular orbit. A rocket going around the spherical Earth in a circular orbit some height above the ground will stay at that height above the ground the entire orbit.

Orbits come down to geometry and traveling sideways really fast. Imagine standing at the edge of a tall cliff overlooking the ocean. If you drop a ball, the ball will fall straight down into the water. If you throw the ball with some sideways speed, the ball will travel in an arc and land a bit further away from the cliff. Now imagine throwing the ball harder and harder with more sideways speed. Each increase in horizontal speed means the ball lands in the water farther from the cliff than before. If you throw the ball hard enough, something weird happens: the amount the ball falls towards the Earth is exactly matched by the amount the spherical Earth curves away from the ball. The net result is that the height of the ball above the water doesn't change—and it will just keep going and going.

Keep in mind that even though it doesn't hit the ground, the ball is actually falling towards the Earth the whole time—it simply never gets closer to the ground since its curved trajectory matches the curvature of the Earth. In other words, the ball is in orbit. Of course, you can't actually get a ball into orbit by throwing it off a cliff like this since air molecules in Earth's atmosphere will slow it down and eventually make it fall to the ground. Which is exactly why rockets also have to travel upwards into space before they can orbit the Earth (Baird, 2013).

ROCKET MATH

Now that we know what it means to get a satellite into orbit, let's think about how scientists and engineers get it there. Think about what determines how big a rocket needs to be to lift a satellite into space and get it moving sideways fast enough to orbit the Earth. To start, let's think about what we have to do to put a person or a satellite into orbit. The answer is that we need to attach a rocket underneath this payload that has enough fuel and power to lift the required mass into orbit.

Can you see why math is so important? The rocket attached to the payload also has fuel, which means we need another rocket under the first that has enough fuel and power to lift it. But, this second rocket we just attached also has some mass (again, mostly its fuel), so we need another rocket to lift it! And on, and on, and on. Even if a rocket's payload is small, it needs a lot of fuel to lift it the sixty-two miles straight up from the ground into space.

There's a math equation that summarizes this whole situation and tells engineers roughly how much fuel is needed to lift a given amount of mass into orbit by a particular rocket. It's called the *rocket equation*. It tells engineers how to calculate the speed gained by a rocket as it burns its fuel. In particular, the equation says that the speed increase is proportional to the mass of the rocket (including the rocket itself, the payload, and all of its fuel) divided by the final mass of the rocket (once all the fuel is burned). This is why rockets have to be enormous (Shortt, 2017).

The rocket equation was essentially the same thing that Katherine Johnson was working on back in the early 1960s. She had to use a lot of hard math to calculate the speed, acceleration, and direction required to hurl a spacecraft of certain size and fuel capacity to hit a moving target (the Moon), without a lot of room for extra maneuvering. It's been compared to trying to hit a rotating bull's-eye with a dart while jumping off a carousel, the dart being the astronaut, the Earth the spinning carousel, and the bull's eye a spot on the Moon.

NASA has an awesome section on their website called Exploring Space Through Math. They have great lessons that give you practice using all kinds of math in connection with space. Scan the QR code to jump over to the site. Don't forget your notebook. That would be a great place to work out the NASA math problems!

MATH IN SPACE

Our universe is so massive. There are multiple orbits coexisting in our universe. The Earth orbits the Sun within the solar system. Our solar system is part of the Milky Way galaxy, which itself orbits a huge black hole at the center. On top of this, the Milky Way galaxy orbits at a gigantic average speed of about 514,000 miles per hour.

At this average speed of 514,000 mph, it takes about 230 million years to complete one rotation. This is called a galactic revolution or galactic year. Therefore, one galactic year ago dinosaurs ruled the Earth. Scientists believe Earth has had around eighteen galactic years in its lifetime (Pultarova and Tillman, 2021).

Math uses numbers. Space has some pretty impressive numbers to describe just how big it is. There is a black hole four million times the size of our Sun at the center of the Milky Way.

Luckily this pit of darkness is 28,000 light years away. Black holes are invisible as the gravity within a black hole is so strong that not even light can get out.

Neptune is another planet in our galaxy that is about two-and-a-half billion miles away, or roughly a twelve year journey. If you could get there you'd be in for a wild experience. Wind speeds on the planet get up to 1,600 mph making it the windiest planet in our solar system. Neptune is known for another crazy number: its moon, Triton, is one of the coldest places in the solar system with a surface temperature of −391 Fahrenheit! (NASAEPDC Editors, 2019)

There's also big math when we talk about how massive our galaxy is. It's so big that scientists don't use miles to describe the distance. Have you heard the phrase "speed of light?" A light year is the distance light travels in one Earth year. Our galaxy has a radius of 52,580 light years. That means if you got in a rocket and traveled across our entire galaxy, it would take you 100,000 years! If we use a more familiar number, we could say the Milky Way is about 621,000,000,000,000,000 miles wide. To put this in perspective, one trip all the way around our Earth at the equator is almost 8,000 miles.

And then we have some cool math going on with our Moon. Every year the Moon moves almost four centimeters further away from the Earth. In 1969, NASA sent the Apollo 11 astronauts to the Moon. They didn't just land on the Moon for the first time, they also set up a really cool experiment. They were trying to determine whether the distance from Earth to the Moon was constant or changing. To do this, the astronauts put mirrors on the Moon's surface that are still there today! Scientists send laser pulses to the mirrors on the Moon to determine the current distance from the Earth to the Moon. Because of this experiment, started fifty-two years ago, scientists have discovered that every year, the Moon moves 3.8 cm further away from the Earth. Even though that doesn't seem like a big distance, over time it adds up! (BBC.com Staff, 2011)

When it comes to the star at the center of our solar system, the Sun has a ton of math to go along with its size. The Sun's mass takes up 99.8 per cent of all the mass of the solar system! Can you imagine? We can fit one million Earths inside the Sun! That's massive and the wild part is the Sun is considered an average-size star. Even though it's 93,000,000 miles away, we still feel its warmth all the way down here on Earth!

Δ

So far in our exploration of different space jobs, we've looked how science, technology, engineering and math all play a vital role when it comes to space. Hopefully you learned some new and exciting lessons about how your school classes are actually helping you prepare for a great career in space!

 Before we go on to the next chapter, check out NASA's awesome STEM Toolkit about Mars. It has a ton of activities for you to try like coding a game and exploring rockets through various simulations. Just scan the QR code and you'll be on your way!

6

Blast Off!

We're going to do some serious pretending in this chapter and get on a rocket and travel all the way up into outer space and all the way out to the International Space Station. From suiting up in your astronaut gear to docking at the ISS, the goal is to give you a realistic feel for just how many things happen to make the space mission successful and let you step into the action of being a real-life astronaut!

LAUNCH DAY

Can you think what the first thing an astronaut does on launch day might be? If you guessed something about the weather, give yourself a gold star. Four hours and fifteen minutes before your flight, you and your crew mates receive a weather briefing. This is an important first step because NASA and SpaceX don't want you rocketing up through high winds, lightning or thunderstorms. When it comes to weather, there are fourteen "Do Not Launch" criteria in all that make sure the astronauts are safe!

Ok, so the weather is good. Now what? Your spacesuit! You and the crew take thirty-eight minutes to suit up at Kennedy Space Center's Neil Armstrong Operations and Checkout Building. Putting all that gear on is definitely not the same as putting on jeans and a t-shirt!

DOI: 10.4324/9781003263104-6

When everyone is ready, you and your crew leave the building and get into the NASA and SpaceX Tesla Model X crew transportation vehicle. You depart the Ops and Checkout building and drive the eight-and-a-half miles to historic Launch Complex 39A. After you arrive, you get out and take the elevator up to the Crew Access Arm that you walk across to reach the Dragon capsule. At two hours, thirty-five minutes until launch you and the other astronauts enter the Dragon!

With only two hours and twenty minutes to launch, you check communications with ground control. Five minutes later, your seats rotate up putting you on your back and in a better position to view the screens and controls. You and your crew check your suits to make sure there are no leaks and that you're good to go. Can you imagine actually being in this position? What a rush!

At the two-hours-to-launch mark, the hatch on your ship is closed and the ground support crew leaves the pad. You are now 240 feet in the air, on your back, facing the sky, adrenaline slowly building. Now it's a waiting game. For fifty minutes, it's you and your thoughts as you wait for the next step in the launch sequence.

When the clock hits one hour and ten minutes to launch, the exact state and location of the International Space Station is uploaded to the computer onboard the Dragon capsule. Twenty-five minutes later, the Go / No Go poll is taken to decide whether your rocket gets fueled up. If all the weather conditions are favorable, you are one step closer to reaching for the stars. With forty-two minutes to launch, the Crew Access Arm is retracted. Things start happening faster now as your mind wonders what it will feel like when the clock hits zero!

What lies below you and your crew in the rocket is truly mind-bending. Five hundred tons of cryogenic propellant sit ready in your vehicle's tanks. Five hundred tons!

A side note: while all this is going on, Navy rescue swimmers wait on warships out in the Atlantic Ocean prepared to rescue you if anything were to go wrong during the rocket's ascent.

Next, the Dragon launch escape system is armed, which gives you the ability to abort from the rocket if there were a problem during fuel up or during ascent.

Thirty-five minutes before blast off, the RP-1 rocket fuel and the cryogenic liquid oxygen are loaded into your rocket's first stage. RP-1 fuel is also loaded into the second stage. Liquid oxygen fills stage one.

Sixteen minutes to launch. Liquid oxygen fills stage two.

Seven minutes and counting, your Falcon 9 begins engine chill.

Two minutes later, Dragon switches to internal power.

One minute to launch. Your command flight computer begins final pre-launch checks. Propellant tank pressurization to flight pressure begins.

Forty-five seconds to go!

SpaceX Launch Director verifies go for launch.

10-9-8-7-6-5-4…

Three seconds left.

Engine controller commands engine ignition sequence to start.

2-1…

LIFT OFF!

It feels like the Earth has exploded beneath you. Your hands grip the armrests. The ground recedes below you as your ship takes off into the ocean blue Florida sky. It's a magical feeling that only a few have experienced. So many thoughts are racing through your mind. You're on your way to the International Space Station, but the middle part of your journey has just begun.

SPACE BOUND

When you've been in the air for two and a half minutes, your first stage main engine cuts off (MECO). Seconds later, the first stage of your rocket separates from the second stage. Your second stage engines fire up. Five minutes later, stage one reenters Earth's atmosphere. At eight minutes, forty-three seconds after launch, your second stage engine cuts off (SECO-1).

Stage one prepares to land on the autonomous spaceport drone ship *Of Course I Still Love You* nine minutes after launch.

At the twelve minute mark, your crew's Dragon capsule separates from the second stage. The Dragon nosecone open sequence begins. After a few checks of the Draco reaction control thrusters and a few pointing maneuvers, there's a phase burn to align the orbits of the Dragon and the International Space Station.

At nine hours and forty-four minutes there's another phase adjustment burn. At eleven hours, ten minutes the Dragon capsule performs a burn using its Draco thrusters to boost its orbit closer to the International Space Station.

Twelve hours in, there's another burn which circularizes the orbit.

Seventeen hours, forty minutes in and after a few mid-course burns, the Dragon is approaching the 400 m keep out sphere and requires a Go / No Go poll from mission control to continue. Ten minutes later your Dragon capsule enters the keep out sphere and hits Waypoint Zero which is 400 m below the ISS.

At eighteen hours, fifteen minutes in you're getting super close! The Dragon capsule arrives at Waypoint 1 and holds approximately 220 m away to align to the docking axis.

A final Go / No Go Poll is given for docking and you arrive at Waypoint 2 which is only twenty meters away from the station! The Dragon capsule departs Waypoint 2 and goes in for the final docking and has contact and capture with the International Space Station.

You made it! All of that took a little over nineteen hours.

Great job!

ABOARD THE ISS

You arrive inside the ISS and are welcomed by other astronauts onboard. You learn that the entire station is actually made up of sixteen pressurized modules: six are from Russia, eight are US modules, two were sent by the Japanese and one is a European module. It's like a gigantic floating puzzle in space. The newest module, *Nauka*, launched July 21, 2021, will become the primary laboratory module on the Russian segment of the space station (NASA, 2022, *International Space Station*).

The Functional Cargo Block was the very first module of the International Space Station to have been launched and provided electrical power, storage, propulsion and guidance to the ISS during the initial stage of assembly. With the launch and assembly in orbit of other modules with more specialized functions, the FCB is now primarily used as a big storage shed.

Pirs was a Russian module on the ISS. *Pirs* was launched on September 14, 2001, and was located on the *Zvezda* module of the station. It provided the ISS with one docking port for Soyuz and Progress spacecraft, and allowed egress and ingress for spacewalks by cosmonauts using Russian Orlan spacesuits. *Pirs* was docked to *Zvezda* for almost twenty years, until July 26, 2021, where it was decommissioned and undocked by Progress MS-16 to make way for the new *Nauka* module.

Zvezda is another module of the International Space Station. It was the third module launched to the station, and provided all of the station's life support systems, some of which are supplemented in the US Orbital Segment, as well as living quarters for two crew members. It is the structural and functional center of the Russian Orbital Segment, which is the Russian part of the ISS. Crew assemble here to deal with emergencies on the station.

Poisk is a docking module of the International Space Station that was added in 2009 and was the first major Russian addition since 2001. *Poisk* is Russian for *explore* or *search* and combines various docking and science capabilities.

Rassvet is a module primarily used for cargo storage and as a docking port for visiting spacecraft. It was flown to the ISS aboard Space Shuttle *Atlantis* on the STS-132 back in May of 2010.

Nauka is the newest module added in July of 2021 and is known as the Multipurpose Laboratory Module. After *Nauka* docked, it began firing its engine thrusters in error, causing the entire space station to make one and a half full rotations before the module ran out of fuel, enabling ground controllers to stop the rotation and the crew to get it back to its original position an hour later.

Onboard, you will also go through seven US modules.

Leonardo, named after Leonardo DaVinci, was flown into space aboard the Space Shuttle *Discovery* on STS-133 on February 24, 2011. *Leonardo* is primarily used for storage of spares, supplies and waste on the ISS, which was until then stored in many different places within the space station. It is also the personal hygiene area for the astronauts who live in the US Orbital Segment.

Harmony is the "utility hub" of the International Space Station. It connects the laboratory modules of the United States, Europe and Japan, as well as providing electrical power and electronic data. Sleeping cabins for four crew members are also housed here. *Harmony* was successfully launched into space aboard Space Shuttle flight STS-120 on 23 October 2007.

Quest, previously known as the Joint Airlock Module, is the primary airlock for the International Space Station. The airlock was launched on STS-104 on July 14, 2001.

Tranquility is another module of the International Space Station. It contains environmental control systems, life support systems, a toilet, exercise equipment and an observation cupola. On February 8, 2010, NASA launched the module on the Space Shuttle's STS-130 mission.

Unity is the first US-built component of the International Space Station. It connects the Russian and United States segments of the station and is where crew eat meals together. The module is cylindrical in shape, with six berthing locations (forward, aft, port, starboard, zenith and nadir) facilitating connections to other modules.

Cupola is an observatory module of the International Space Station. Its name derives from the Italian word *cupola*, which means "dome." Its seven windows are used to conduct experiments, dockings and observations of Earth. It was launched aboard Space Shuttle *Endeavor*'s mission STS-130 on February 8, 2010.

Destiny, also known as the US Lab, is the primary operating facility for US research payloads aboard the International Space Station. *Destiny* is NASA's first permanent operating orbital research station since Skylab back in 1974. *Destiny* launched on February 7, 2001 aboard the Space Shuttle *Atlantis* on STS-98. Astronauts work inside this pressurized facility to conduct research in a lot of different scientific fields. Scientists throughout the world use the results to enhance their studies in medicine, engineering, biotechnology, physics, materials science and Earth science.

Moving on, you will find two Japanese modules. The first *Kibō*, which means "hope," is a science module. It is the largest single ISS module, and is attached to the *Harmony* module. The first two pieces of the module were launched on Space Shuttle missions STS-123 and STS-124. The third and final components were launched on STS-127.

The second is called the Pressurized Module which is the core component connected to the port hatch of *Harmony*. It is cylindrical in shape and contains twenty-three International Standard Payload Racks, ten of which are dedicated to science experiments while the remaining thirteen are dedicated to *Kibō*'s systems and storage. The end of the PM has an airlock and two window hatches. This is also the location for many of the press conferences that take place on board the station.

Finally, the single European module is called the *Columbus* which is another science laboratory on board the station and is the largest single contribution to the ISS made by the European Space Agency. It was launched aboard Space Shuttle *Atlantis* on February 7, 2008, on flight STS-122. The European Space Agency spent roughly two billion dollars on building *Columbus*, including the experiments it carries and the ground control infrastructure necessary to operate them.

Congratulations!

You and your crew will spend a few weeks at the ISS before returning home. It's a journey only a handful of people have made.

7

Who's Who?

Now let's take a brief look at some influential men and women in the space industry and their backgrounds. There are tons of people who have done great things when it comes to space. If we were talking about a Hall of Fame list of space people, that list would include Elon Musk, Neil deGrasse Tyson, Sara Seager, Liu Yang and Steve Squyres.

ELON MUSK

Elon Musk is a South African-born American entrepreneur and businessman who founded X.com in 1999 (which later became PayPal), SpaceX in 2002 and Tesla Motors in 2003. Musk became a multimillionaire in his late twenties when he sold his start-up company, Zip2, to a division of Compaq Computers (Biography. com Editors, 2014, *Elon Musk*).

Musk made headlines in May 2012, when SpaceX launched a rocket that would send the first commercial vehicle to the International Space Station. Since then, SpaceX has launched three crewed missions up to the ISS!

Early Life
Musk was born on June 28, 1971, in Pretoria, South Africa. As a child, Musk was so lost in his daydreams about inventions that his parents and doctors ordered a test to check his hearing. When

DOI: 10.4324/9781003263104-7

he was ten, Musk developed an interest in computers. He taught himself how to program, and when he was twelve he sold his first software game he created called Blastar.

In grade school, Musk was short, introverted and loved to study. He was actually bullied until he was fifteen and went through a growth spurt and learned how to defend himself with karate and wrestling.

Family

Musk's mother, Maye Musk, worked five jobs at one point to support Elon and the rest of her family. Musk's father, Errol Musk, is a wealthy South African engineer. Elon spent his early childhood with his brother Kimbal and sister Tosca in South Africa.

Education

At age 17, in 1989, Elon moved to Canada to attend Queen's University and avoid mandatory service in the South African military. Musk obtained his Canadian citizenship that year, in part because he felt it would be easier to obtain American citizenship that way.

In 1992, he left Canada to study business and physics at the University of Pennsylvania. He graduated with an undergraduate degree in economics and stayed for a second Bachelor's degree in Physics.

After leaving Penn, Elon headed to Stanford University in California to pursue a PhD in energy physics. However, his move was timed perfectly with the Internet becoming a huge thing, and he dropped out of Stanford after just two days to become a part of it, launching his first company in 1995.

Companies

Zip2 Corporation

Musk started his first company, Zip2 Corporation, with his brother Kimbal. An online city guide, Zip2 was soon providing content for the new websites of both *The New York Times* and the *Chicago Tribune*. In 1999, a division of Compaq Computer Corporation bought Zip2 for $307 million in cash and $34 million in stock options!

PayPal

In 1999, Elon and Kimbal Musk used the money from their sale of Zip2 to found X.com, an online financial services / payments company. An X.com acquisition the following year led to the creation of PayPal as it is known today.

In October 2002, Musk earned his first billion when PayPal was acquired by eBay for $1.5 billion in stock.

SpaceX

Musk founded his third company, Space Exploration Technologies Corporation, or SpaceX, in 2002 with the intention of building spacecraft for commercial space travel. By 2008, SpaceX was well established, and NASA awarded the company the contract to handle cargo transport for the International Space Station—with plans for astronaut transport in the future—in a move to replace NASA's own space shuttle missions.

Falcon 9 Rockets: On May 22, 2012, Musk and SpaceX made history when the company launched its Falcon 9 rocket into space with an unmanned capsule. The vehicle was sent to the International Space Station with 1,000 pounds of supplies for the astronauts stationed there, marking the first time a private company had sent a spacecraft to the International Space Station.

In December 2013, a Falcon 9 successfully carried a satellite to geosynchronous transfer orbit, a distance at which the satellite would lock into an orbital path that matched the Earth's rotation. In February 2015, SpaceX launched another Falcon 9 fitted with the Deep Space Climate Observatory (DSCOVR) satellite, aiming to observe the extreme emissions from the Sun that affect power grids and communications systems on Earth.

In March 2017, SpaceX saw the successful test flight and landing of a Falcon 9 rocket made from reusable parts, a development that opened the door for more affordable space travel.

The company enjoyed another milestone moment in February 2018 with the successful test launch of the powerful Falcon Heavy rocket. Armed with additional Falcon 9 boosters, the Falcon Heavy was designed to carry immense payloads into orbit and potentially serve as a vessel for deep space missions.

For the test launch, the Falcon Heavy was given a payload of Musk's cherry-red Tesla Roadster, equipped with cameras to "provide some epic views" for the vehicle's planned orbit around the Sun.

Starlink Internet Satellites: In late March 2018, SpaceX received permission from the US government to launch a fleet of satellites into low orbit for the purpose of providing Internet service. The satellite network, named Starlink, would ideally make broadband service more accessible in rural areas, while also boosting competition in heavily populated markets that are typically dominated by one or two providers.

SpaceX launched the first batch of sixty satellites in May 2019, and followed with another payload of sixty satellites that November. While this represented significant progress for the Starlink venture, the appearance of these bright orbiters in the night sky, with the potential of thousands more to come, worried astronomers who felt that a proliferation of satellites would increase the difficulty of studying distant objects in space.

Tesla Motors

Musk is the co-founder, CEO and product architect at Tesla Motors, a company formed in 2003 that is dedicated to producing affordable, mass-market electric cars as well as battery products and solar roofs. Musk oversees all product development, engineering and design of the company's products.

Roadster: Five years after its formation, in March 2008, Tesla unveiled the Roadster, a sports car capable of accelerating from 0 to 60 mph in 3.7 seconds, as well as traveling nearly 250 miles between charges of its lithium ion battery.

Model S: In August 2008, Tesla announced plans for its Model S, the company's first electric sedan that was reportedly meant to take on the BMW 5 series. In 2012, the Model S finally entered production at a starting price of $58,570. Capable of covering 265 miles between charges, it was honored as the 2013 Car of the Year by *Motor Trend* magazine.

In April 2017, Tesla announced that it surpassed General Motors to become the most valuable US car maker (Biography.com Editors, 2014, *Elon Musk*).

NEIL DEGRASSE TYSON

One of America's best-known scientists, astrophysicist Neil de-Grasse Tyson, has spent much of his career sharing his knowledge with others. He has a great talent for presenting complex concepts in a clear and accessible manner (Biography.com Editors, 2014, *Neil deGrasse Tyson*).

After studying at Harvard University, he earned his doctorate from Columbia University in 1991. Tyson went to work for the Hayden Planetarium in 1996 before becoming its director. Additionally, he has served as host of *NOVA ScienceNow* and the *StarTalk Radio* podcast. Tyson remains a popular TV science expert today.

Early Life and Education

Born in New York City on October 5, 1958, Tyson discovered his love for the stars at an early age. When he was nine, he took a trip to the Hayden Planetarium at the Museum of Natural History where he got his first taste of star-gazing. Tyson later took classes at the Planetarium and got his own telescope. As a teenager, he would watch the skies from the roof of his apartment building.

An excellent student, Tyson graduated from the Bronx High School of Science in 1976. He then earned a Bachelor's degree in Physics from Harvard University and a doctorate in astrophysics from Columbia University in 1991. After spending a few years doing postdoctorate work at Princeton University, Tyson landed a job at the Hayden Planetarium.

Career Highlights

Director of the Hayden Planetarium

Tyson eventually became the director of the Hayden Planetarium and worked on an extensive renovation of the facility, assisting with its design and helping raise the necessary funds. The $210 million project was completed in 2000, and the revamped site offered visitors a cutting-edge look at astronomy. One of Tyson's most controversial decisions at the time was the removal of Pluto from the display of planets. He classified Pluto as a dwarf planet, which invoked a strong response from some visitors. While some asked for the planet Pluto back, the International Astronomical Union followed Tyson's lead in 2006. The organization officially labeled Pluto as a dwarf planet.

Host of NOVA ScienceNow

In addition to his work at the planetarium, Tyson has found other ways of improving the nation's understanding of science. "One of my goals is to bring the universe down to Earth in a way that further excites the audience to want more," he once said. Tyson has taken his message to the airwaves, serving as the host of the *NOVA ScienceNow* documentary series from 2006 to 2011. In addition to breaking down barriers between scientists and the general public, Tyson has brought diversity to astrophysics. He is one of the few African Americans in his field.

Presidential Advisor to George Bush

Tyson has also served as a presidential advisor. In 2001, President George W. Bush appointed the astrophysicist to a commission on the future of the aerospace industry. Tyson also served on another commission three years later to examine US policy on space exploration.

Celebrity Scientist and TV Appearances

These days, Tyson is one of the most in-demand science experts. He gives talks across the country and is a media favorite whenever there is an important science issue in the news. Tyson is known for his ability to make difficult concepts accessible to every audience, his great speaking skills and his sense of humor, which has led to appearances on such shows as *Real Time with Bill Maher*, *The Colbert Report* and *The Daily Show*.

SARA SEAGER

Professor Seager was born and grew up in Toronto, Canada. Among her first memories is a trip to a "star party" with her father, to see the Moon through a telescope! Professor Seager graduated from the Jarvis Collegiate Institute, a 200-year old public high school known for its science education. During high school she was astounded to learn that one could be an astrophysicist for a living, only to be deterred by her father, who believed the best career was as a doctor or lawyer.

Seager entered the University of Toronto with the idealistic view that anything and everything could be described by a physics equation. She soon learned that, in reality, approximations are not only rampant but necessary. This realization motivated Professor Seager to eventually leave pure physics to pursue her "first love," astronomy. After graduating with a BSc in the Math and Physics Specialist Program at the University of Toronto, Seager attended the PhD program in Astronomy at Harvard.

While at Harvard in the mid-1990s, the first reports of exoplanets around Sun-like stars began appearing. Encouraged by her PhD supervisor, Dimitar Sasselov, Seager studied the atmospheres of these so-called hot Jupiter planets. At the time, many scientists were skeptical of the new planets, preferring to believe they were the result of a different phenomenon, such as star variability. Others thought the claims made in Seager's thesis would never be substantiated. But exoplanets kept turning up and Seager's early work was eventually validated.

In 1999, Professor Seager joined the group of postdoctoral fellows at the Institute for Advanced Study in Princeton, NJ. There, she benefited enormously from the mentorship of the late John Bahcall. Unlike most scientists at the time, John Bahcall supported Seager's new ideas in exoplanets with almost unbounded enthusiasm, as long as the underlying physics was sound and the phenomenon was detectable some day in Seager's lifetime. Bahcall's support enabled Seager to initiate several new topics in exoplanet characterization.

Professor Seager's research now focuses on theoretical models of atmospheres and interiors of all kinds of exoplanets as well as novel space science missions. Her research has introduced many new ideas to the field of exoplanet characterization, including work that led to the first detection of an exoplanet atmosphere. She was part of a team that co-discovered the first detection of light emitted from an exoplanet and the first spectrum of an exoplanet.

Today, Professor Seager is an astrophysicist and planetary scientist at MIT. She lives with her husband and two sons in Massachusetts (MIT Department of Physics, 2022).

LIU YANG

Chinese astronaut and fighter pilot Liu Yang became the first woman from China to reach outer space (Gregersen, 2021). The first American woman who traveled to space was Sally Ride, in 1983, at the age of 32.

Life in China
Liu Yang was born in China on October 6, 1978 and out of 500 million Chinese women, Liu Yang was chosen to be the country's first space heroine. She had no siblings and lived in Beijing with her parents.

Astronaut Training
When Liu Yang finished high school, one of her teachers persuaded her to join the People's Liberation Army Air Force. She did so and, by 1997, she had already logged 1,680 flight hours. She graduated from the Aviation University of the Chinese Air Force. She was classified as a pilot and became deputy chief of a flight unit, with the rank of Major.

In addition to her skills as a pilot, Liu Yang's superiors praised her displays of courage and composure under difficult circumstances. It is very likely that if Liu Yang had lived in the 1930s, she would have wanted to emulate the American aviator Amelia Earhart.

In May 2010, Liu Yang was recruited as a pilot in China's select group of future astronauts or taikonauts. After two years of arduous training, she excelled in the tough selection tests. She was a candidate to man the Shenzhou-9 spacecraft. Liu Yang traveled to space with two companions and the news quickly became the most popular on Chinese Twitter, with 33 million posts. Echoing a famous Chinese proverb, the spokeswoman added: "Women hold up half the sky. Human space missions without women are incomplete."

STEVE SQUYRES

Steven Squyres is a geologist and astronomer who has worked extensively for NASA. He returned to Cornell University after five years to become a professor of astronomy, but has still been involved in assisting with various space missions.

His interests include the history of water on Mars, the geophysics of the icy satellites of the outer planets, and the tectonics of Venus. Squyres was an associate of the Voyager imaging science team, a radar investigator for the Magellan mission to Venus, and a co-investigator for the 1996 Russian Mars mission, and his research projects include the Gamma-Ray Spectrometer Investigation for the 2001 Mars Surveyor Mission, the Mars Express High Resolution Stereo Camera (HRSC) Investigation, Mars Exploration Rovers (MER), Spirit and Opportunity, the Cassini Imaging Science Subsystem and participation in the HIRISE mission.

In *Roving Mars: Spirit, Opportunity, and the Exploration of the Red Planet*, Squyres recounts the work that led to the Mars Exploration Rover mission, a landmark in his career. He recalls the setbacks and successes experienced by teams of scientists and engineers who spent long hours working out the details that culminated in success, so much so that the robotic rovers, Spirit and Opportunity, that landed in 2004 continued to send back data far beyond the end of the mission. The success of the mission returned energy and enthusiasm to NASA, which had suffered several setbacks in the preceding years, including the deaths of several astronauts. The mission proved that water once flowed on the surface of Mars, which meant that life may have once existed there (Encyclopedia.com Editors, 2022).

YOU

These famous people are only a small handful of men and women who dedicated their lives to studying space in one way or another. Did one of them stand out to you? Why? You, too, can achieve the same goals if you work hard to develop your talents.

In the next chapter we will take a look at some cool job opportunities you may have when you graduate college.

ASTRONAUT

It takes years of studying and training to become an astronaut, and most begin when they're aged between twenty-seven and thirty-seven. To work for the NASA, you'll need to have at least a degree in engineering, biological science, physical science or math—ideally an advanced degree too. You'll also need to have clocked up at least 1,000 hours piloting a jet aircraft, so many astronauts come from a military background. You'll also need to be in excellent shape (you'll have to do a physical test).

SPACESUIT DESIGNER

A spacesuit designer is usually a highly trained engineer with a speciality in mechanical engineering and, of course, an interest in space. Spacesuit designers take into consideration the requirements of each specific mission and design their suits accordingly.

8

A Universe of Opportunities

Space flight is already developing beyond NASA missions; companies like SpaceX and Boeing, for example, are looking specifically for astronauts. Also, with commercial space tourism slowly edging into common consciousness, there will be a significant increase in the need for shuttle-steering space pilots. Virgin Galactic, for example, is such a company, aiming to transform the current cost, safety and environmental impact of space launches.

The most obvious job to do with space that comes to mind is astronaut. So, if you dream about setting sail into the galaxy, this could be the job for you. However, it's important to bring you back down to Earth and note that the majority of an astronaut's career is spent on firm ground, training, preparing and supporting other astronauts on missions.

Of the thousands of young people who dream of becoming an astronaut, only a handful will make it to this job, but that doesn't mean that you should lose heart as there are plenty of other exciting jobs in space that you can do, even if you don't make it to Mars.

For example, the European Space Agency offers a Young Graduate Trainee program for graduates who want a career in space—this is aimed at engineers, physicists, biologists, lawyers, and medical and business graduates.

DOI: 10.4324/9781003263104-8

Most importantly, they've got to make sure the astronauts are kept alive and comfortable. One example is the special fabric used to soak up the sweat of astronauts during long spacewalks. Well, no one said it was glamorous.

PAYLOAD SPECIALIST

You've definitely heard of astronauts, but did you know that flying to space is only one part of their job description? A payload specialist is an astronaut who's in charge of the scientific experiments aboard a space mission. As trained scientists in varying fields, payload specialists make sure experiments are conducted safely and correctly in order to get accurate results.

They spend their time observing experiments, recording data, and liaising with scientists back on Earth. Some examples of the experiments they've conducted include 3D printing in zero gravity and exposing yeast to space radiation.

SPACE LAWYER

Ok, this one isn't exactly what it sounds like. Space lawyers aren't really lawyers in space. Instead, they take care of all the legal stuff from down on the ground. Usually experts in international law, they are often faced with questions like "Who is responsible if two satellites collide?" or "Who owns the minerals on an asteroid?" With the future of space tourism on the horizon, they are now tasked with writing laws to protect both passengers and companies in the unpredictable world of outer space.

You won't get to handle legal disputes in space, but the job of space lawyer is still open to all space buffs or those interested in advising the government or private companies.

There are only four universities that teach space law in the world, but two of them are in the US, at the University of Mississippi School of Law and University of Nebraska–Lincoln's Doctor of Juridical Science.

Michelle Hanlon, Professor of Aviation and Space Law at the University of Mississippi, told USA Today that there are two types of space lawyers: the traditional academic, who can be a professor or international representative, and the newer role of adviser to companies like SpaceX. In addition to teaching international and domestic administrative law, Hanlon is the co-founder of law firm For All Moonkind, which she says focuses on preserving humans' heritage in space.

"When you think about preserving our history, we have about fifty-five space lawyers working with us to talk about how we're going to protect those sites," she said. "Legally, we need to figure out how to get them recognized in the same way we recognize the pyramids or Stonehenge. We don't have a mechanism to do that in space yet" (Aspegren, 2019).

EDUCATOR ASTRONAUT

Can you imagine your chemistry teacher floating around in zero gravity? Well, that's what NASA calls an educator astronaut. These are teachers and other education professionals who have been trained to fly into space like any other astronaut. Tasked with teaching classrooms from space, the aim of these unique astronauts is to get kids passionate about careers in science, technology, engineering and mathematics. Most importantly, they are meant to inspire the next generation of space explorers all the way from Earth's orbit!

SPACE RESEARCHER

Traveling into space is no mean feat. It has a huge impact on an astronaut's body and is fraught with challenges like low gravity and radiation exposure. Space medicine looks at the biological, physiological and psychological effects of space flight on humans and how gravity (or lack of it) affects us.

Doctors and medical researchers work very hard to make sure that astronauts are kept safe and healthy during their long trips into space. They also do valuable research which can actually be used to improve the health of us earthlings on firm ground too.

There are a few universities in the UK which specialize in space medicine. For example, University College London has a Centre for Space Medicine and Kings College London offers an MSc (Master of Science) in Space Physiology and Health.

Δ

Going to space might not be too far off for some, thanks to a renewed commitment by NASA to return astronauts to the Moon by 2024 and private companies like SpaceX launching rockets seemingly every week.

But astronauts soon won't be the only ones going to space. Space tourism is growing into a major market. And with the likes of Virgin Galactic and Blue Origin competing in a space race, the stars might not be so out of reach.

Here are some more jobs that may sound like science fiction now but aren't far off from becoming mainstream.

SPACE ARCHEOLOGIST

There are other jobs that are actively safeguarding human space heritage: space historians, curators and archaeologists. Space historians have long had a place in preserving artifacts from the Apollo and other space missions for the public.

There is a demand to send archeologists and anthropologists up to the Moon to piece together and preserve human history in space. The sites host valuable artifacts for archeologists and anthropologists who want to study humanity's growing space heritage. However, in order to become Space Indiana Jones, as with many jobs on this list, you have to go to school first and get at least a Bachelor's degree.

SPACE DOCTOR

Why do your forehead and eyes change shape after a year in space? What do days, weeks, months or even years away from Earth in space mean for a person psychologically? How long would you actually survive if you were stranded on Mars?

A number of universities, including King's College London, seek to answer these questions through space physiology and health programs through "training for biomedical scientists and doctors with an interest in the biomedical issues associated with space exploration" (Aspegren, 2019).

These Master's programs are becoming more applicable by the day. The Mars Desert Research Station (MDRS) runs simulations of space-like events for scientists in "Mars"—or an environment like it, Utah—and is geared toward researching the human challenges to a space mission.

SPACE MINER

There are approximately 9,000 known asteroids traveling in orbit close to the Earth, and 1,000-odd new ones are discovered each year, according to NASA. A company called Planetary Resources is looking to harness these space rocks, which its website says can "make it possible to fuel and sustain life in space, creating a new paradigm of travel and human presence in space."

According to NASA, the minerals that lie in the belt of asteroids between Mars and Jupiter hold wealth equal to a staggering $100 billion for every person on Earth.

But there is more to space mining than a gold rush for the sci-fi age. Taking mining off Earth could help relieve humanity's destruction of our planet's environment. "There are an estimated two trillion tons of water available on near-Earth asteroids," says the company on their website. "This water can be used to sustain human life and as propellant for spacecraft."

The Colorado School of Mines offers a variety of retraining courses for adults to get certified in this new field.

SPACE METEOROLOGIST

Space meteorology is already somewhat of an influential area. According to the American Meteorological Society, space weather occurs because emissions from the Sun influence the space environment around Earth, as well as other planets. "Accurate space weather prediction could save society hundreds of millions of dollars a year," said AMS in a 2008 statement, by monitoring the

 Earth's ozone layer, climate change, and overall air pollution to help society make necessary changes to keep the environment safe. "The need for accurate forecasting only increases. Forecasters continually monitor the space environment using both space- and ground-based assets and issue alerts and warnings of a likely impact on Earth (Aspegren, 2019).

Before we move on, there is a great YouTube channel called "Everyday Astronaut" that gives you everything you need to know about all the current events that are going on in the space world! Just scan the QR code and check out all the cool and awesome things going on in the aerospace industry.

9

But Wait, There's More!

We've covered so much information on space your head might be spinning right about now. The goal of this chapter is to give you some other things to think about. We're going to look at some cool stuff that scientists have found in our solar system and hopefully create an even bigger interest for you about investigating some of them when you grow up.

As you read, don't forget about your notebook where you can take some notes and see if you can come up with a list of your top three favorite concepts that we've investigated. That way you will be able to focus your energy for our last chapter which deals with what you can take in high school and what colleges offer what degree plans regarding specific space careers.

Let's take a look at some cool facts about our solar system, the Milky Way galaxy and the universe beyond to see just what else might spark your imagination and curiosity. Who knows, after all is said and done you might create your own career path!

THE SOLAR SYSTEM

The solar system is a bizarre place with its alien planets, mysterious moons and strange phenomena that are so out-of-this-world they escape explanation. Scientists have discovered ice-spewing volcanoes on Pluto, while Mars is home to a truly "grand"

DOI: 10.4324/9781003263104-9

canyon the size of the United States. There may even be a giant, undiscovered planet lurking somewhere beyond Neptune.

Let's look at some of the strangest facts about planets, dwarf planets, comets and other incredible objects around the solar system.

THE SUN

While the Sun's visible surface—the photosphere—is 10,000 degrees Fahrenheit (5,500 degrees Celsius), the upper atmosphere has temperatures in the millions of degrees. It's a large temperature differential with little explanation, for now.

NASA has several Sun-gazing spacecraft on the case, however, and they have some ideas for how the heating is generated. One is "heat bombs," which happens when magnetic fields cross and realign in the corona. Another is when plasma waves move from the Sun's surface into the corona.

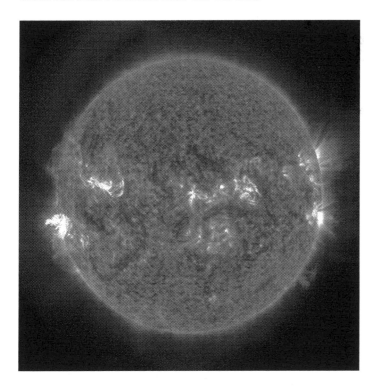

URANUS

Uranus appears to be a featureless blue ball upon first glance, but this gas giant of the outer solar system is pretty weird upon closer inspection. First, the planet rotates on its side for reasons scientists haven't quite figured out. The most likely explanation is that it underwent one or more titanic collisions in the ancient past. In any case, the tilt makes Uranus unique among the solar system planets.

Uranus also has tenuous rings, which were confirmed when the planet passed in front of a star (from Earth's perspective) in 1977; as the star's light winked on and off repeatedly, astronomers realized there was more than just a planet blocking its starlight. More recently, astronomers spotted storms in Uranus' atmosphere several years after its closest approach to the Sun, when the atmosphere would have been heated the most.

One of the most bizarre moons in the outer solar system is Miranda, which, unfortunately, we saw only once when Voyager 2 passed by it in 1986. This moon of Uranus has bizarre features on its surface, with sharp boundaries separating ridges, craters and other things. It is possible that the moon could have had tectonic activity, but how that happened on a body with a diameter of 500 km is a mystery (Howell, 2017).

Scientists aren't sure how the patchwork surface came about, and we likely won't be able to tell for sure until another mission gets out there. Perhaps the moon was smashed into bits and coalesced again, or maybe meteorites struck the surface and caused temporary melts in small areas.

JUPITER

The Sun and the planets likely formed from the same cloud of hydrogen and helium gas. This would especially be true of Jupiter, a planet 317 times the size of Earth that pulled in a lot more gas than our own planet. So if that's the case, why does Jupiter have more heavy, rocky elements than the Sun?

One of the leading theories is that Jupiter's atmosphere is "enriched" by the comets, asteroids and other small rocky bodies that it pulls in with its strong gravitational field. Since amateur telescopic technology has improved, several small bodies have been seen falling into Jupiter in the past decade. Along with being the solar system's largest planet, Jupiter also hosts the solar system's largest storm. Known as the Great Red Spot (since it's big and ruddy-colored), it's been observed in telescopes since the 1600s. Nobody knows exactly why the storm has been raging for centuries, but in recent decades another mystery emerged: the spot is getting smaller.

In 2014, the storm was only 10,250 miles (16,500 km) across, about half of what was measured historically. The shrinkage is being monitored in professional telescopes and also by amateurs, as telescope and computer technology allow high-powered photographs at an affordable cost. Amateurs are often able to make more consistent measurements of Jupiter, because viewing time on larger, professional telescopes is limited and often split between different objects (Howell, 2017).

For those of us used to Earth's relatively simple moon, the chaotic landscape of Jupiter's moon Io may come as a huge surprise. The Jovian moon has hundreds of volcanoes and is considered the most active moon in the solar system, sending plumes up to 250 miles into its atmosphere.

Some spacecraft have caught the moon erupting; the Pluto-bound New Horizons craft caught a glimpse of Io bursting when it passed by in 2007. Io's eruptions come from the immense gravity the moon is exposed to, being nestled in Jupiter's gravitational well. The moon's insides tense up and relax as it orbits closer to, and farther from, the planet, generating enough energy for volcanic activity. Scientists are still trying to figure out how heat spreads through Io's interior, though, making it difficult to predict where the volcanoes are located using scientific models alone.

MARS

While Mars seems quiet now, we know that in the past something caused gigantic volcanoes to form and erupt. This includes Olympus Mons, the biggest volcano ever discovered in the solar system. At 374 miles (602 km) across, the volcano is comparable to the size of Arizona. It's sixteen miles (twenty-five kilometers) high, or triple the height of Mount Everest, the tallest mountain on Earth.

Volcanoes on Mars can grow to such immense size because gravity is much weaker on the Red Planet than it is on Earth. But how those volcanoes came to be in the first place is not well known. There is a debate as to whether Mars has a global plate tectonic system and whether it is active.

If you thought the Grand Canyon was big, that's nothing compared to Valles Marineris. At 2,500 miles (4,000 km) long, this immense system of Martian canyons is more than ten times as long as the Grand Canyon on Earth. Valles Marineris escaped the notice of early Mars spacecraft (which flew over other parts of the planet) and was finally spotted by the global mapping mission Mariner 9 in 1971.

The lack of active plate tectonics on Mars makes it tough to figure out how the canyon formed. Some scientists even think that a chain of volcanoes on the other side of the planet, known as the Tharsis Ridge, somehow bent the crust from the opposite side of Mars, thus creating Valles Marineris. More close-up study is needed to learn more, but you can't send a rover over there easily.

Methane is a substance that is produced by life (such as by microbes) or by natural processes such as volcanic activity. But why it keeps fluctuating so much on Mars is a mystery. Various telescopes and space probes have found different levels of methane on Mars over the years, making it hard to chart where this substance is coming from. It's unclear if the varying levels of methane are due to telescopic differences, or differences in the amount of methane coming from the surface.

NASA's Curiosity rover even detected a spike in methane during one Martian year that did not repeat the next, indicating whatever it saw was not seasonal. It will likely take more long-term observations of Mars to fully figure out the mystery.

VENUS

Venus is a burning-hot planet with a high-temperature, high-pressure environment on its surface. Scientists have found that its upper winds flow fifty times faster than the planet's rotation. The European Venus Express spacecraft (which orbited the planet between 2006 and 2014) tracked the winds over long periods and detected periodic variations. It also found that the hurricane-force winds appeared to be getting stronger over time.

Water ice was once considered a rare substance in space, but now we know we just weren't looking for it in the right places. In fact, it exists all over the solar system. Ice is a common component of comets and asteroids, for example. But we know that not all ice is the same. Close-up examination of Comet 67P/Churyumov–Gerasimenko by the European Space Agency's Rosetta spacecraft, for example, revealed a different kind of water ice than what is found on Earth (Howell, 2017).

That said, ice has been found in permanently shadowed craters on Mercury and the Moon, although we don't know if there's enough to support colonies in those places. Mars also has ice at its poles, in frost and likely below the surface dust. Even smaller bodies in the solar system have ice—Jupiter's moon Europa, Saturn's moon Enceladus, and the dwarf planet Ceres, among others.

We've been exploring space for more than sixty years, and have been lucky enough to get close-up pictures of dozens of celestial objects. Most notably, we've sent spacecraft to all of the planets in our solar system—Mercury, Venus, Earth, Mars, Jupiter, Saturn, Uranus and Neptune—as well as two dwarf planets, Pluto and Ceres.

The bulk of the flybys came from NASA's twin Voyager spacecraft, which left Earth in 1977 and are still transmitting data from beyond the solar system in interstellar space. Between them, the Voyagers clocked visits to Jupiter, Saturn, Uranus and Neptune, thanks to an opportune alignment of the outer planets.

So far, scientists have found no evidence that life exists elsewhere in the solar system. But as we learn more about how "extreme" microbes live in underwater volcanic vents or in frozen environments, more possibilities open up for where they could live on other planets. These aren't the aliens people once feared lived on Mars, but microbial life in the solar system is a possibility.

Microbial life is now considered so likely on Mars that scientists take special precautions to sterilize spacecraft before sending them over there. That's not the only place, though. With several icy moons scattered around the solar system, it's possible there are microbes somewhere in the oceans of Jupiter's Europa, or perhaps underneath the ice at Saturn's Enceladus, among other locations.

For many years, scientists believed that Earth was the only tectonically active planet in the solar system. That changed after the Mercury Surface, Space Environment, Geochemistry and Ranging (MESSENGER) spacecraft did the first orbital mission at Mercury, mapping the entire planet in high definition and getting a look at the features on its surface.

In 2016, data from MESSENGER (which had crashed into Mercury as planned in April 2015) revealed cliff-like landforms known as fault scarps. Because the fault scarps are pretty small, scientists are sure that they weren't created that long ago and that the planet is still contracting 4.5 billion years after the solar system was formed.

SATURN

While we've known about Saturn's rings since telescopes were invented in the 1600s, it took spacecraft and more powerful telescopes built in the last fifty years to reveal more. We now know that every planet in the outer solar system—Jupiter, Saturn, Uranus and Neptune—each have ring systems. That said, rings are very different from planet to planet. Saturn's spectacular rings, which may have come from a broken-up moon, are not repeated anywhere else. Rings aren't limited to planets, either. In 2014, for example, astronomers discovered rings around the asteroid Chariklo. Why such a small body would have rings is a mystery, but one hypothesis is perhaps a broken-up moonlet created the fragments (Howell, 2017).

Another weird moon in Saturn's system is Titan, which hosts a liquid "cycle" that moves between the atmosphere and the surface. That sounds a lot like Earth, until you begin looking at its environment. It has lakes filled with methane and ethane, which could be reminiscent of the chemistry that occurred on Earth before life arose.

Saturn's northern hemisphere has a raging six-sided storm nicknamed "the hexagon." Why exactly it's that shape is a mystery. But what is known is that this hexagon, which shares several features in common with hurricanes, has been there for at least several decades—if not hundreds of years.

Lighting conditions in Saturn's northern hemisphere began to improve in 2012, when Saturn approached its northern summer solstice. Cassini spent twenty years observing the wonders of Saturn until the end of its mission in 2017, when it took a final plunge into the giant planet's atmosphere.

COMETS

Comets used to be the province of amateur astronomers, who spent night after night scouring the skies with telescopes. While some professional observatories also made discoveries while viewing comets, this really began to change with the launch of the Solar and Heliospheric Observatory (SOHO) in 1995.

Since then, the spacecraft has found more than 2,400 comets, which is incredible considering its primary mission is to observe the Sun. These comets are nicknamed "sungrazers" because they come so close to the Sun. Many amateurs still participate in the search for comets by picking them out from raw SOHO images. One of SOHO's most famous observations came when it watched the breakup of the bright Comet ISON in 2013 (Howell, 2017).

In January 2015, California Institute of Technology astronomers Konstantin Batygin and Mike Brown announced—based on mathematical calculations and simulations—that there could be a giant planet lurking far beyond Neptune. Several teams are now on the search for this theoretical "Planet Nine," which could take decades to find (if it's actually out there).

This large object, if it exists, could help explain the movements of some objects in the Kuiper Belt, an icy collection of objects beyond Neptune's orbit. Brown has already discovered several large objects in that area that in some cases rivaled or exceeded the size of Pluto. (His discoveries were one of the catalysts for changing Pluto's status from planet to dwarf planet in 2006.)

NEPTUNE

Neptune is far away from Earth, and you can bet that scientists would love to get another spacecraft out there sometime soon. Perhaps today's technology could better answer some Neptunian mysteries, such as why the blue planet is giving off more heat than it receives. It's bizarre, considering that Neptune is so far away from the Sun.

Scientists would love to know what's going on, because it's believed that the vast temperature differential could affect weather processes on the planet. NASA estimates the temperature difference between the heat source and the cloud tops is 260 degrees Fahrenheit (160 degrees Celsius) (Howell, 2017).

EARTH

Earth has bands of radiation belts surrounding our planet, known as the Van Allen belts (named after the scientist who discovered this phenomenon). While we've known about the belts since the dawn of the space age, the Van Allen Probes (launched in 2012) have provided our best-ever view of them. They've uncovered quite a few surprises along the way.

Scientists now know that the belts expand and contract according to solar activity. Sometimes the belts are very distinct, and sometimes they swell into one massive belt. An extra radiation belt (beyond the known two) was spotted in 2013. Understanding these belts helps scientists make better predictions about space weather, or solar storms.

What in this chapter caught your attention? Is there a particular part of our galaxy that you are interested in? If you had to the opportunity to investigate/explore one thing in space what would it be? Put your answer in your journal. Maybe find a sticky note and mark the page. Come back to your "one thing" and add notes and ideas. As you think about a possible career in space, this particular entry may fuel your future goals and pursuits.

10

Get a Job!

We've come to the end of our journey and the beginning of yours. Before we go, let's look at a few areas that will keep you interested both in current space events as well as future missions. To keep you busy after school and on the weekends, scan the QR code to find a ton of cool NASA activities that will help you continue exploring space in fun ways.

HIGH SCHOOL

When you get to high school you will start having the opportunity to take classes that help build a good knowledge base for your career in space. High school students interested in studying aerospace engineering should take courses in chemistry, physics and mathematics, including algebra, trigonometry and calculus. If you're thinking about being an astronaut, you need to take algebra, astronomy, biology, computer applications, physical science and physics. You can see the overlap in courses like physics and algebra. Another tip is to try and take Advanced Placement versions of these classes because a lot of high schools will give you college credit when you pass them!

Get involved. Whether it's a sport or band, becoming a part of a group helps you hone your communication skills and gives you the opportunity to work with others.

DOI: 10.4324/9781003263104-10

COLLEGE

Next comes college. In this section we will explore a list of colleges that offer degrees that will open doors for your space career as well as what colleges have related space programs based on specific interests (US News Editors, 2022).

The top colleges that have produced the most **astronauts** include:

1 University of California–Berkeley
2 University of California–Los Angeles
3 University of Washington–Seattle
4 Auburn University–Auburn
5 University of Illinois–Urbana-Champaign
6 University of Texas–Austin
7 Stanford University–Stanford
8 University of Colorado–Boulder
9 Massachusetts Institute of Technology–Cambridge
10 Purdue University–West Lafayette
11 United States Military Academy–West Point
12 United States Air Force Academy–Colorado
13 United States Naval Academy–Annapolis

The colleges with the best **aerospace engineering** programs include (in order of rank) (US News Editors, 2022):

1 California Institute of Technology–Pasadena
2 Massachusetts Institute of Technology–Cambridge
3 Stanford University–Stanford
4 Georgia Institute of Technology–Atlanta
5 University of Michigan–Ann Arbor
6 Purdue University–West Lafayette
7 University of Illinois–Urbana-Champaign
8 University of Texas–Austin
9 Texas A&M University–College Station
10 Cornell University–Ithaca
11 Princeton University–Princeton
12 University of Colorado–Boulder

Another area of working with a company like SpaceX or NASA is computing and the technology needed to blast a rocket into space and bring it back again. These careers require degrees in computer science, information systems / IT or engineering. The colleges with the best **computer science degree programs** include (in order of rank) (US News Editors, 2022):

1 Carnegie Mellon University–Pittsburgh
2 Massachusetts Institute of Technology–Cambridge
3 Stanford University–Stanford
4 University of California–Berkeley
5 University of Illinois–Urbana-Champaign
6 Cornell University–Ithaca
7 University of Washington–Seattle
8 Georgia Institute of Technology–Atlanta
9 Princeton University–Princeton
10 University of Texas–Austin
11 California Institute of Technology–Pasadena
12 University of Michigan–Ann Arbor
13 Columbia University–New York
14 University of California–Los Angeles

It's cool to see that a lot of the same colleges are on more than one of the lists! Sometimes people like to go to college close to home, while others don't mind going to a college far away in order to get the right education that matches their interests. It would be fun if you printed out a map of the United States and find where you live and then use three different colors to mark the "astronaut" colleges, the "aerospace" colleges, and the "computer science" colleges. That will give you a great visual and a way to figure out just how near or far away the colleges are from where you currently live!

…AND BEYOND

Finally, we've come to the end of our Earth-bound journey through space. Be encouraged to revisit your notebook and add to your drawings and take more notes as you continue on your way through school. As you grow in knowledge, always be thinking ahead for solutions to problems. Consider how you can use your life to connect humans to the infinite reaches of space.

You have been created to do great things. Use this book as a resource to revisit and keep learning about space. Keep drawing and writing about your ideas in your space notebook. You never know when they'll come in handy. Keep reading and researching. You are special and unique. You see things in ways that no one else does.

Take this guide to the cosmos and dream about all the ways you can help others connect with space. You're going to be amazed at what you can accomplish. Don't let anyone tell you you're not old enough or smart enough. Work hard in school and along the way look for connections between what you're learning and what you know about space.

Neil Armstrong, the first person to walk on the Moon, said, "That's one small step for a man, one giant leap for mankind." Your time in school learning your subjects are the small steps on your journey to an epic career in space. Your future creations and inventions will be the giant leap that will take people everywhere to unknown places beyond the stars. It's exciting, isn't it?

You've got this.

Go and shine like the stars.

Good luck!

Works Cited

Anthony, Erin. *Research and Technology*. NASA, January 21, 2022. Web.

Aspegren, Elinor. *Space Jobs on the Rise*. USA Today, July 22, 2019. Web.

Baird, Christopher. *Why Doesn't the Earth Fall Down?* Wtamu. edu, July 1, 2013. Web.

BBC.com Staff. *Why the Moon Is Getting Further Away From Earth*. BBC.com, February 1, 2011. Web.

Biography.com Editors. *Elon Musk*. Biography.com, April 2, 2014. Web.

Biography.com Editors. *Neil deGrasse Tyson*. A&E Television Networks, April 2, 2014. Web.

Encyclopedia.com Editors. "Squyres, Steven 1957–." *Encyclopedia.com*, January 25, 2022. Web.

Earth Data. *What is Remote Sensing?* December 6, 2021. Web.

Garcia, Mark. *Artemis*. NASA, July 9, 2022. Web.

Gregersen, Erik. "Liu Yang." *Encyclopedia Britannica*, September 27, 2021. Web.

Howell, Elizabeth. *25 Weirdest Facts about the Solar System*. Space. com, February 15, 2017. Web.

Lehman, Mildred K. and Lehman, Milton. "Robert Goddard." *Encyclopedia Britannica*, October 1, 2021. Web.

MIT Department of Physics. *Sara Seager*. MIT, 2022. Web.

NASA. *About Edwin Hubble*. NASA, 2022. Web.

NASA. *International Space Station*. NASA, 2022. Web.

NASAEPDC Editors. *10 Interesting Facts about Neptune*. Tx-state-epdc.net, November 1, 2019. Web.

Pultarova, Tereza and Tillman, Nola. *Milky Way Galaxy*. Space. com, December 3, 2021. Web.

Shortt, David. *Learn the Rocket Equation*. The Planetary Society, April 28, 2017. Web.

Smithsonian.com Editors. *Humans in Space*. Airandspace.si.edu, 2022. Web.

Squyres, Steven. *Roving Mars*. Hachette Books, 2006.

Stanzione, Kaydon Al. "Aerospace Engineering." *Encyclopedia Britannica*, March 8, 2019. Web.

Tillman, Nola. *Kaplana Chawla*. Space.com, February 10, 2022. Web.

US News Editors. *Best National University Rankings*. 2022. www.usnews.com/best-colleges/rankings/national-universities

Wall, Mike. *Nearby Alien Planets Not So Life Friendly After All*. Space.com, April 24, 2015. Web.

Wikitronics. *CMOS*. electronics.fandom.com, 2022. Web.

Wilson, Jim. *Missions*. NASA, January 21, 2022. Web.

Printed in the United States
by Baker & Taylor Publisher Services